Suzuki

CELLO SCHOOL

Volume 2
Cello Part
Revised Edition

© 2007, 1978 Dr. Shinichi Suzuki
Sole publisher for the entire world except Japan:
Summy-Birchard, Inc.
Exclusive print rights administered by
Alfred Publishing Co., Inc.
All rights reserved.   Printed in USA.

ISBN 0-87487-481-5

INTRODUCTION

FOR THE STUDENT: This volume is part of the worldwide Suzuki Method of teaching. The companion recording should be used along with this publication. A piano accompaniment book is also available for this material.

FOR THE TEACHER: In order to be an effective Suzuki teacher, ongoing education is encouraged. Each regional Suzuki association provides teacher development for its membership via conferences, institutes, short-term and long-term programs. In order to remain current, you are encouraged to become a member of your regional Suzuki association, and, if not already included, the International Suzuki Association.

FOR THE PARENT: Credentials are essential for any Suzuki teacher you choose. We recommend you ask your teacher for his or her credentials, especially those related to training in the Suzuki Method. The Suzuki Method experience should foster a positive relationship among the teacher, parent and child. Choosing the right teacher is of utmost importance.

In order to obtain more information about the Suzuki Association in your region, please contact:

International Suzuki Association
www.internationalsuzuki.org

CONTENTS

© 1979 Fritz Henle

Maestro Pablo Casals

Photograph by Lawrence Block

The four main points for study in Volume II:

1. The child should listen to the reference recordings every day at home to develop musical sensitivity. Rapid progress depends on this listening.

2. Tonalization, or the production of a beautiful tone, should be stressed in the lesson **and** at home.

3. The position etudes should be practiced well before each lesson.

4. Constant attention should be given to accurate intonation, correct posture, and the proper bow hold.

Tonalization

Each lesson should begin with a tonalization.
Try to produce a beautiful tone. Use full bows.

Maintain the same volume and intensity throughout each bow stroke.

Ringing Sound Tonalization

*Listen for ringing sound.

1 Long, Long Ago

Moderato

T. H. Bayly

Variation

2 May Time

W. A. Mozart

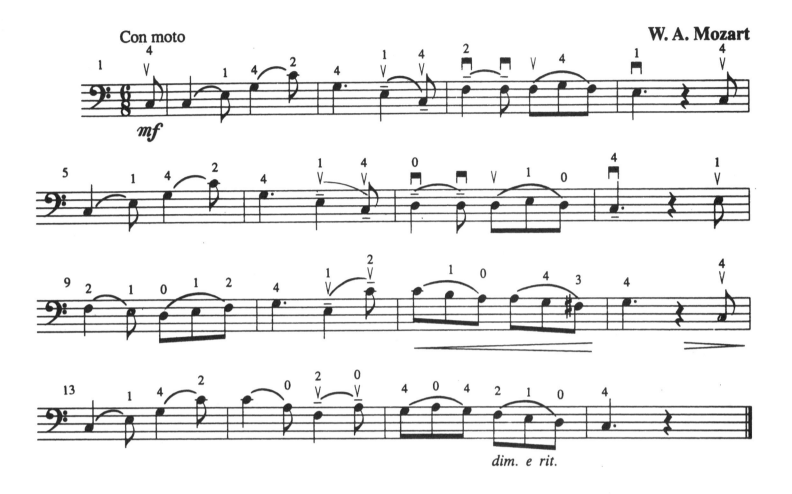

Con moto

mf

dim. e rit.

Etudes for 2nd Position

Closed hand position is marked with ○.
Open hand position is marked with ×.

Forward and backward extension using 2nd position.

Tonalization

3 Minuet No. 1

J. S. Bach

* Practice slowly and accurately in the beginning.

Shift quickly.   Practice to increase speed and accuracy.

4 Minuet No. 3

J. S. Bach

5 Chorus from "Judas Maccabaeus"

G. F. Handel

Please remember that the child should listen to the recording every day.

Ear Training

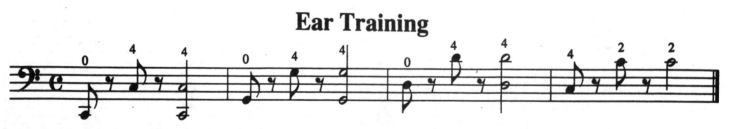

Exercise for perfect octave intonation. Listen to the resonance of the open C, G, and D strings, and try to match the octave pitches perfectly.

6 Hunters' Chorus

C.M. von Weber

7 | Musette from English Suite No. 3

J. S. Bach

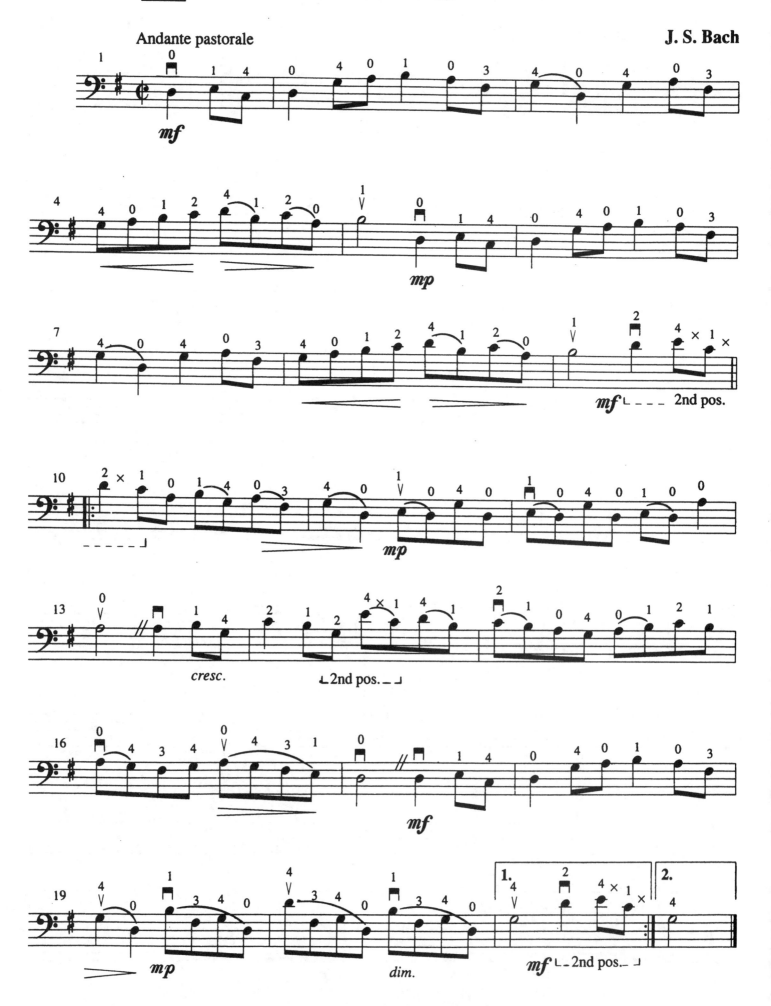

8 March in G

J. S. Bach

9 Theme from "Witches' Dance"

N. Paganini

Exercise for B♭

Try playing the following exercise silently. Keep second finger in place as the first finger moves back from B♮ to B♭.

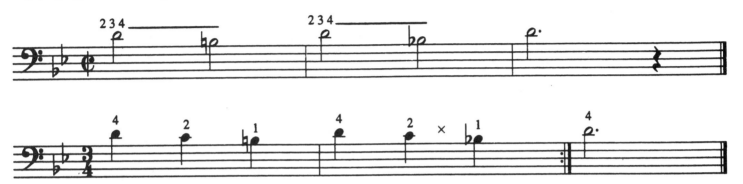

Practice Twinkle Theme in F major to prepare left hand for backward extension.

Tonalization

The Moon over the Ruined Castle

R. Taki

10 The Two Grenadiers

R. Schumann

11 Gavotte

F. J. Gossec

For asterisked passages, see next page.

D.C. al Fine

Preparation Exercises for Gossec Gavotte

Procedure for practice:

Listen carefully to the intonation.
Use a short stroke.
Place the bow on the string, then play, keeping the bow on the string during the rest.

****Pluck the string with a finger of the right hand.

12 Bourrée

G. F. Handel

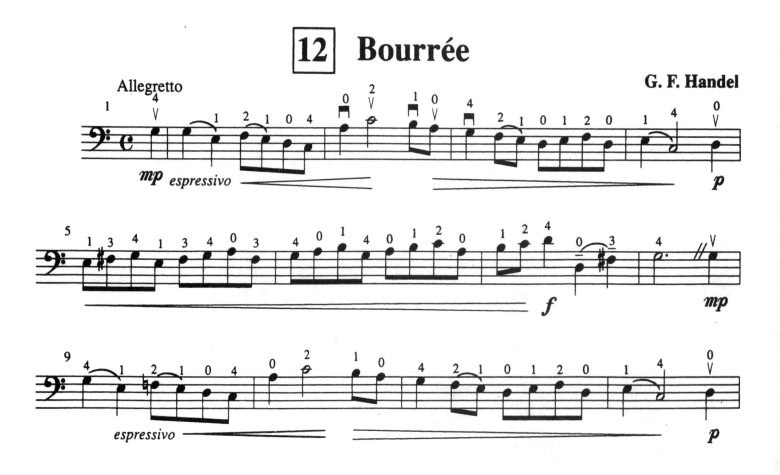